About Skill Builders Word Problems

by Carolyn Chapman

Welcome to RBP Books' Skill Builders series. Like our Summer Bridge Activities collection, the Skill Builders series is designed to make learning both fun and rewarding.

Students often ask parents and teachers, "When am I ever going to use this?" Skill Builders Word Problems books have been developed to help students see the uses of math in the world around them. Exercises help students develop problem-solving skills in real-world situations while increasing confidence in their math skills.

Content is based on current NCTM (National Council of Teachers of Mathematics) standards and supports what teachers are currently using in their classrooms. Word Problems can be used both at school and at home to engage students in problem solving.

The fifth-grade math skills in this book include addition, subtraction, multiplication, division, graphing, fractions, measurement, money values, and time. Special emphasis is given to multistep problems.

A critical thinking section includes exercises to help develop higher-order thinking skills.

Learning is more effective when approached with an element of fun and enthusiasm—just as most children approach life. That's why the Skill Builders combine entertaining and academically sound exercises with eye-catching graphics and fun themes—to make reviewing basic skills at school or home fun and effective, for both you and your budding scholars.

www.summerbridgeactivities.com

Table of Contents

Sweet Treats

Solve each problem.

Sam buys 83 pieces of licorice, 32 gumdrops, and 49 jawbreakers. How many pieces of candy does he buy altogether?

$$\begin{array}{r} {}^{1} \\ 83 \\ 32 \\ +\ 49 \\ \hline 164 \end{array}$$

164 pieces of candy

1. Jan makes 67 orange chocolates, 36 mint chocolates, and 98 caramel chocolates. How many chocolates does she make altogether?

2. Alex boxes 65 plain candy bars, 98 peanut candy bars, and 44 caramel candy bars. What is the total number of candy bars Alex boxes?

3. Tyler buys 77 pounds of sugar, 69 pounds of butter, and 21 pounds of flour. How many pounds of ingredients does Tyler buy altogether?

4. Hank sells 93 packages of licorice, 28 boxes of lemon drops, and 75 candy bars. How many pieces of candy does Hank sell altogether?

Shoe Sense

Solve each problem.

Rick sold 478 pairs of shoes in April, 873 pairs in May, and 377 pairs in June. How many pairs of shoes did Rick sell altogether?

$$\begin{array}{r} {\scriptstyle 2\,1} \\ 478 \\ 873 \\ +\ 377 \\ \hline 1{,}728 \end{array}$$ **pairs of shoes**

1. The Big Foot shoe factory produced 649 sneakers, 493 sandals, and 908 boots. How many shoes did they produce altogether?

2. The Sneaker Division at the Big Foot shoe factory produced 293 red sneakers, 938 yellow sneakers, and 830 white sneakers. How many sneakers did they produce altogether?

3. Amber cut 823 inches of shoelace on Monday, 382 inches of shoelace on Tuesday, and 744 inches of shoelace on Wednesday. How many inches of shoelace did she cut altogether?

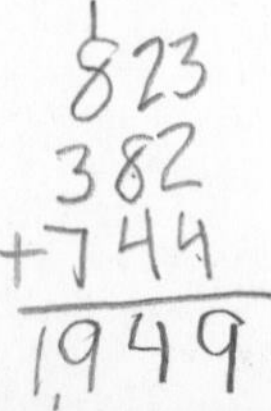

4. Hanna boxed 584 bottles of black shoe polish, 481 bottles of brown shoe polish, and 632 bottles of blue shoe polish. What is the total number of bottles Hanna boxed?

Shoe Sense

Solve each problem.

1. Eric folded 8,464 shoe boxes, and Ryan folded 7,392 shoe boxes. How many shoe boxes did Eric and Ryan fold altogether?

2. Lizzie boxed 698 boxes of pink flip-flops, 488 boxes of green flip-flops, and 741 boxes of blue flip-flops. How many flip-flops did Lizzie box altogether?

3. The Boot Division at the Big Foot shoe factory produced 4,399 black boots, 8,832 brown boots, and 149 red boots. What was the total number of boots produced?

4. Jeff stuffed 458 shoes with tissue paper. Dexter stuffed 893 shoes with tissue paper. How many shoes did Jeff and Dexter stuff altogether?

Bookworms

Anne's class kept track of the number of pages they read for the last 3 months. Use the information in the table to work each problem.

Student	Number of Pages Read
Josh	4,125
Keshia	3,698
Kristy	3,547
Abe	2,977
Caroline	2,558
Anne	1,798

How many total pages did Anne and Caroline read?

```
  1 11
  1,798
+ 2,558
  4,356  pages
```

1. How many pages did Josh and Abe read altogether?

2. How many more pages did Josh read than Kristy?

3. How many pages did Anne and Keshia read altogether?

4. If Caroline's books have 4,322 pages total, how many more pages does she have left to read?

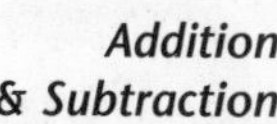

Bookworms

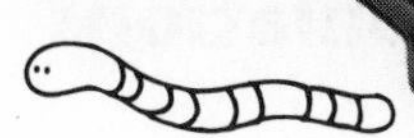

Use the information in the table on page 6 to work each problem.

1. How many pages less did Abe read than Kristy?

2. How many pages did Kristy and Keshia read altogether?

3. If Anne's books have 2,382 pages, how many more pages does she have left to read?

4. How many pages did the girls read altogether?

People Populations

Solve each problem. The first problem is worked for you.

City	Population in 1990	Population in 2000
Newport Beach, California	66,643	70,032
Palo Alto, California	55,900	58,598
Englewood, Colorado	29,396	31,727
Miami Beach, Florida	92,639	87,933
Jackson, Mississippi	202,062	184,256
Jackson, Tennessee	49,145	59,643

How many more people lived in Jackson, Mississippi, than in Jackson, Tennessee, in 2000?

```
  7 13 1
 184,256
– 59,643
 124,613  more people
```

1. How many more people lived in Englewood in 2000 than in 1990?

2. In 2000, how many people lived in Palo Alto and Newport Beach altogether?

People Populations

Use the table on page 8 to solve each problem.

1. Which 2 cities' population decreased in the year 2000?

2. In 1990, how many more people lived in Miami Beach than Englewood?

3. Which city in California had the greatest increase in population in 2000?

4. In 1990, how many people lived in Miami Beach, Jackson, and Jackson altogether?

Forest Fun

Solve each problem.

Shawn saw 182 birds, 377 squirrels, and 87 deer. How many animals did Shawn see altogether?

```
 2 1
 182
 377
+ 87
----
 646 animals
```

1. Anita saw 582 pink wildflowers, 499 purple wildflowers, and 257 orange wildflowers. How many wildflowers did Anita see altogether?

2. Camp Winnemucca used 789 paper cups, 1,393 napkins, and 867 paper plates. How many supplies did they use altogether?

3. Four hundred sixty-six squirrels live in the forest. If 299 chipmunks also live in the forest, how many squirrels and chipmunks are there altogether?

4. In August, 3,571 campers visited the park. The park had 1,773 campers in September and 977 campers in October. How many campers visited the park in the three months altogether?

Forest Fun

Solve each problem. The first problem is worked for you.

Seven hundred forty-two campers were at the campground during the last 3 months. There were 238 campers in July and 389 campers in August. How many campers were there in June?

238 (carries 1 1)	(campers in July)	742 (4 crossed out to 3, carry 1)	(total campers)
+ 389	(campers in August)	– 627	(campers in July & August)
627	campers in July & August	115	campers in June

1. Maria took 548 pictures. She took 112 pictures of wildflowers, 89 of trees, and 56 of mountains. The rest were pictures of animals. How many pictures of animals did Maria take?

2. Alex hiked with 688 campers. Two hundred fifteen campers had cameras. Three hundred seventy-two campers had binoculars. How many campers didn't have cameras or binoculars?

3. Jamie put up 632 tents in a week. She put up 289 tents on Monday and 218 on Tuesday. How many tents did she put up the rest of the week?

4. Camp Winnemucca used 2,280 bags of marshmallows during the last 6 months. They used 438 bags in May, 382 in June, 299 in July, and 185 in August. How many bags did they use the rest of the months?

Meatballs at Mario's

Solve each problem.

Mario used 329 cans of tomato sauce in one week. He used 37 cans on Monday, 49 cans on Tuesday, and 25 cans on Wednesday. How many cans of tomato sauce did he use the rest of the week?

37 (cans on Monday)	
49 (cans on Tuesday)	**329** (cans used for the week)
+ 25 (cans on Wednesday)	**– 111** (cans used Mon.–Wed.)
111 total cans used Mon.–Wed.	**218** cans of tomato sauce

1. Mario owns an Italian restaurant. On Monday, he made 67 meatballs. On Tuesday, he made 74 meatballs. If Mario made 384 meatballs during the week, how many meatballs did he make the rest of the days?

2. One thousand seven hundred eighty-one people ate at Mario's last month. There were 211 customers the first week, 424 customers the second week, and 344 customers the third week. How many customers did Mario have during the rest of the month?

3. Mario served 118 meals during dinnertime. Thirty-two customers ordered lasagna. Forty-nine customers ordered spaghetti, and the rest of his customers ordered pizza. How many customers ordered pizza?

4. Gary spent $65.95 at the restaurant. He spent $37.41 on pizza and $16.25 on salads. He spent the rest on sodas. How much did he spend on sodas?

Meatballs at Mario's

Solve each problem.

1. Mario used 465 pounds of pasta in 6 months. He used 85 pounds in October, 78 pounds in November, and 39 pounds December. How many pounds of pasta did he use the rest of the months?

2. Emma spent $6.25 for spaghetti and meatballs, $1.12 for a soda, and $3.75 for a piece of cake. If Emma paid with a $20.00 bill, how much change did she get back?

3. Mario used 265 loaves of bread in one week. He used 45 loaves on Monday, 58 loaves on Tuesday, and 31 loaves on Wednesday. How many loaves of bread did he use the rest of the week?

4. Mario has $14.35 left in his wallet. He spent $148.43 for napkins. Then he spent $92.05 for table-cloths. How much did Mario have in his wallet to start with?

Ticket Time

Solve each problem.

Sam sold 4 times as many basketball tickets as baseball tickets. If he sold 263 baseball tickets, how many basketball tickets did he sell?

$$\begin{array}{r} {}^{2\,1} \\ 263 \\ \underline{\times\ 4} \\ 1{,}052 \end{array}$$ **basketball tickets**

1. Erica bought 9 times as many carnival tickets as Ben. Ben bought 489 carnival tickets. How many tickets did Erica buy?

2. Marcy sold 3 times as many tickets as Kelsey. Kelsey sold 5,939 tickets. How many tickets did Marcy sell?

3. Karen sold 6 times as many tickets to the fundraiser as Brittany. If Brittany sold 548 tickets, how many tickets did Karen sell?

4. Rock-o-Rama sold 8 times as many tickets in June as they did in May. They sold 4,833 tickets May. How many tickets did they sell in June?

Ticket Time

Solve each problem.

In July, the zoo sold 4 times as many tickets as they did in June. The zoo sold 384 tickets in June. How many tickets did the zoo sell altogether?

$$\begin{array}{r} {}^{3\,1} \\ 384 \\ \underline{\times\ 4} \\ 1{,}536 \end{array}$$ **tickets sold in July**

$$\begin{array}{r} {}^{1\,1} \\ 1{,}536 \\ \underline{+\ 384} \\ 1{,}920 \end{array}$$

1,536 (tickets sold in July)
+ 384 (tickets sold in June)
1,920 tickets sold in all

1. Two hundred thirty-nine people bought movie tickets on Friday. On Saturday, 8 times more people bought movie tickets. How many people bought movie tickets altogether?

2. Jackson sold 5 times as many tickets to the fair as Emily. Emily sold 193 tickets. How many more tickets did Jackson sell than Emily?

3. Emmett bought 6 times as many tickets at the carnival as Ginger. Kim bought 157 tickets. Ginger bought 277 tickets. How many tickets did Emmett, Kim, and Ginger buy altogether?

4. In March, 4,832 train tickets were sold. In April, 3 times as many tickets were sold as in March. How many train tickets were sold altogether?

Cool Collectors

Solve each problem.

1. At the antique store, Grace spends $495.58 for a vase. Cameron spends $242.69 less than Grace for another vase. How much does Cameron spend?

2. Alicia spends $143.92 for a scooter. Kim spends $68.17 for skates. How much more does Alicia spend than Kim?

3. Webster has 1,349 baseball cards. He gives 249 cards to his brother. How many cards does Webster have left?

4. Allison buys a painting for $3,299. Jack buys a painting for $4,342. How much more does Jack spend for his painting than Allison?

Cool Collectors

Solve each problem.

Savannah has 8 times as many CDs in her music collection as Russ. If Russ has 183 CDs, how many more CDs does Savannah have than Russ?

183 (carry 6 2)	**(Russ's CDs)**	1,464 (regroup 3 1)	**(Savannah's CDs)**
x 8		– 183	**(Russ's CDs)**
1,464	**Savannah's CDs**	**1,281**	**more CDs in Savannah's collection**

1. Alan has 5 times more blue marbles than red marbles in his collection. If Alan has 749 red marbles, how many marbles does he have altogether?

2. Garrett collects stamps. He buys a stamp for $142.28. He also buys a rare stamp that costs 4 times as much as the first stamp he bought. How much does Garrett spend altogether?

3. Megan collects 6 times as many aluminum cans to recycle as Max. Max collects 3,429 aluminum cans. How many cans did Megan and Max collect for recycling altogether?

4. Harry buys a model car kit for $64.98. Then he spends 3 times as much on supplies to build the model car. How much does Harry spend altogether?

Party Planners

Solve each problem.

1 tablespoon = 3 teaspoons 1 pint = 2 cups 1 quart = 2 pints 1 gallon = 4 quarts 1 pound = 16 ounces	Misha uses 18 teaspoons of sugar in her lemonade. How many tablespoons does she use? 18 ÷ 3 = **6** tablespoons of sugar

1. Kyle buys 24 pints of ice cream. How many 1-cup servings does he have?

2. Bryan needs 16 gallons of punch for his party. The punch he buys is only sold in quart bottles. How many quarts of punch should he buy?

3. Leslie needs 48 ounces of chocolate for a cake she's making. How many pounds of chocolate should she buy?

4. Quinn has 4 quarts of root beer. How many 1-cup servings does he have?

Party Planners

Solve each problem.

1 tablespoon = 3 teaspoons
1 pint = 2 cups
1 quart = 2 pints
1 gallon = 4 quarts
1 pound = 16 ounces

1. Lisa is making pizza for her friends. If her recipe calls for 64 ounces of cheese, how many pounds should she use?

2. Brandon is making apple cider. If he has 6 quarts, how many 1-cup servings can he pour?

3. If Jenny has 6 gallons of chocolate syrup, how many pints does she have?

4. Shannon has 8 quarts of soup. If she serves each guest 1 cup, how many servings does she have?

Buying and Selling

Solve each problem.

Emma sold 14 times as many candy bars as Kristen. Kristen sold 49 candy bars. How many candy bars did Emma sell?

$$\begin{array}{r} \overset{3}{49} \\ \underline{\times\ 14} \\ 196 \\ \underline{+\ 490} \\ 686 \end{array}$$ **candy bars**

1. Amy sold 24 times as many pizzas as Chris. Chris sold 58 pizzas. How many pizzas did Amy sell?

2. Henry bought 37 nails. If Jackson bought 62 times as many nails as Henry, how many nails did he buy?

3. Tyler sold 16 times as many baseballs as baseball bats. If Tyler sold 92 baseball bats, how many baseballs did he sell?

4. Kim bought 18 times as many stickers as Jen. If Jen bought 93 stickers, how many stickers did Kim buy?

Buying and Selling

Solve each problem.

1. Lisa sold 64 times as many T-shirts as Josie. If Josie sold 74 T-shirts, how many T-shirts did Lisa sell?

2. The toy store sold 71 times as many cars as airplanes. They sold 118 airplanes. How many cars did the toy store sell?

3. Kaylee's mom bought 16 times as many diapers as jars of baby food. If she bought 29 jars of baby food, how many diapers did she buy?

4. The bookstore sold 59 times as many books as magazines. If the bookstore sold 88 magazines, how many books did they sell?

Super Shoppers

Solve each problem using the price tags for each item.

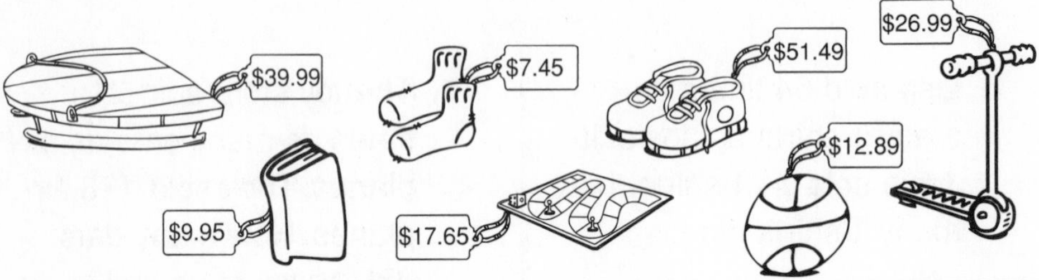

Gary buys a basketball and a board game. How much does he spend altogether?

```
   1 1 1
  $12.89
+ $17.65
  $30.54
```

1. Max buys a sled. Todd buys a scooter. How much more does Max spend than Todd?

2. Lynne buys a pair of tennis shoes and 2 pairs of socks. How much does she spend altogether?

3. Victor has $60.00 in his wallet. He buys a basketball and a sled. How much does he have left?

4. Nicole buys 2 books and a board game. Sara buys a scooter and a basketball. How much more does Sara spend than Nicole?

Super Shoppers

Solve each problem using the price tags on page 22 for each item.

1. Maggie buys a book. Jeff buys a pair of socks. How much more does Maggie spend than Jeff?

2. Kara buys a pair of tennis shoes and a board game. She pays with $80.00. How much change does she get back?

3. Natalie buys 3 board games. Marisa buys 4 pairs of socks. How much more does Natalie spend than Marisa?

4. Caroline buys a basketball and 2 sleds. How much does she spend altogether?

In the City

Remember...
The ***perimeter*** *is the distance around a figure. To find the perimeter of a figure, add the length of each side of the figure.*

Alan is building bookshelves around the perimeter of the reading room in the library. If the reading room is 15 feet by 27 feet, how many feet does he have to work with?

15 + 15 + 27 + 27 = 84 feet

1. The city is putting a cement sidewalk around the playground in the park. If the playground measures 58 feet by 83 feet, how many feet will the sidewalk measure?

2. Rachell is sewing trim around a curtain for the theater. The curtain measures 254 inches by 493 inches. How many inches of trim will she need?

3. At practice, George's coach had the team run around the perimeter of the court 4 times. If the court measures 45 feet by 29 feet, how many feet did the team run?

4. Lucas is fencing a garden on his rooftop. Two of the sides are 15 feet, and the other two sides are 28 feet. How much fencing will Lucas need? If fencing costs 7 cents per foot, how much will he spend?

In the Country

Remember...
*The **perimeter** is the distance around a figure. To find the perimeter of a figure, add the length of each side of the figure.*

Solve each problem.

1. Ben is fencing an area for his cows. Two of the sides are 135 feet long, and the other two sides are 147 feet long. How much fencing does Ben need?

2. Emilee is buying trim to go around her quilt. If two of the edges are 108 inches and the other two edges are 90 inches, how many inches of trim will she need?

3. Samantha is planting her fields. She plants two areas. The first area measures 62 feet by 84 feet. The second area measures 79 feet by 58 feet. What is the perimeter of the areas altogether?

4. Charley is fencing an area for his horses that measures 302 feet by 492 feet. How many feet of fencing will Charley need? If fencing costs $.25 per foot, how much will it cost Charley?

Fix-up Fun

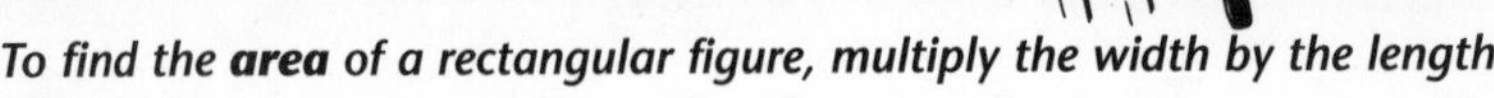

*To find the **area** of a rectangular figure, multiply the width by the length.*

Work each problem.

Cory is carpeting the bedroom. If the floor is 11 feet by 14 feet, how many square feet of carpet will he need?

$$\begin{array}{r} 11 \\ \underline{\times\ 14} \\ 44 \\ \underline{+\ 110} \\ 154 \end{array}$$ **square feet**

1. Lori measures a window for a new piece of glass. The window measures 36 inches wide and 48 inches tall. What is the area of the window?

2. Grayson is working on his roof. The space he is fixing measures 210 inches by 84 inches. What is the area of his roof?

3. Emilee is painting her wall. If the wall measures 12 feet by 23 feet, how many square feet does she paint?

4. George is planting a new lawn. His yard is 34 feet by 52 feet. How many square feet of turf will he need?

Fix-up Fun

Work each problem.

1. Jack is tiling his bathroom floor. His floor measures 98 inches by 89 inches. How many square inches of tile will he need?

2. Denise is painting an area that is 22 feet by 38 feet. How many pints of paint will she need to buy if 1 pint covers 9 square feet?

3. Emilee is carpeting two rooms. The first room is 26 feet by 11 feet, and the second room measures 36 feet by 19 feet. How many square feet of carpet will Emilee need altogether?

4. Linus fertilizes his backyard that is 43 feet wide and 39 feet long. If one bag of fertilizer covers 9 square feet, how many bags of fertilizer will Linus need?

Packaging Produce

Work each problem.

Allison bags oranges. She puts 5 oranges in each bag. If she has 635 oranges, how many bags can she fill?

127 bags

$$\begin{array}{r} 127 \\ 5\overline{)635} \\ \underline{-5} \\ 13 \\ \underline{-10} \\ 35 \\ \underline{-35} \\ 0 \end{array}$$

1. Allie packages apples in bags. She puts 9 apples in each bag. If she has 891 apples, how many bags can she make?

2. Rob packs pineapples in crates. He has 483 pineapples. If he puts 7 pineapples in each crate, how many crates will he need?

3. Lori has 279 cantaloupes. She puts 9 cantaloupes in each box. How many boxes will she need?

4. Rex puts radishes in bunches. If he puts 7 radishes in each bunch, how many bunches can he make with 546 radishes?

Packaging Produce

Work each problem.

1. Keith packages tomatoes in 6-packs. He has 156 tomatoes. If the store sells a 6-pack of tomatoes for $.65, how much will they make selling all of the tomatoes?

2. Pam is sorting lemons and limes. She puts 4 lemons and 2 limes in each bag. If she has 532 lemons and 295 limes, how many bags can she make? How many limes will be left over?

3. The grocery store is selling avocados in bunches of 5. If they have 983 avocados, how many bunches can they sell? How many will be left over?

4. Todd bags fruit. He has 483 oranges, 822 apples, 199 pears, and 552 bananas. If he puts 8 pieces of fruit in each bag, how many bags can he make?

Boxing at the Bakery

Work each problem.

Sara bags rolls. She puts 9 rolls in each bag. If she has 1,492 rolls, how many bags can she make?

165 bags with 7 left over

$$
\begin{array}{r}
165 \\
9\overline{)1{,}492} \\
\underline{-9} \\
59 \\
\underline{-54} \\
52 \\
\underline{-45} \\
7
\end{array}
$$

1. Denise is packaging cookies. She puts 5 cookies in each package. If she has 7,414 cookies, how many packages can she make?

2. Rob puts donuts in boxes. He has 4,932 donuts. If he puts 6 donuts in each box, how many boxes will he need?

3. Rachell has 3,902 bagels. If she puts 8 bagels in each box, how many boxes can she make?

4. Carlos has 1,294 cups of frosting. If each cake he frosts uses 2 cups of frosting, how many cakes can he frost?

Boxing at the Bakery

Work each problem.

1. George has 2,392 glazed donuts, 908 chocolate donuts, and 382 spice donuts. If he puts 9 donuts in each box, how many boxes can he make?

2. Emilee has 4,932 hamburger rolls. She sells 1,294. If she packages the rest and puts 8 in each package, how many packages can she make?

3. Lori makes 2,392 chocolate chip cookies and 3,483 oatmeal cookies. If she puts 9 cookies in each container, how many containers can she make?

4. George bakes 2,120 cinnamon rolls. He puts 4 rolls in each box. If he sells each box for $1.49, how much does he earn?

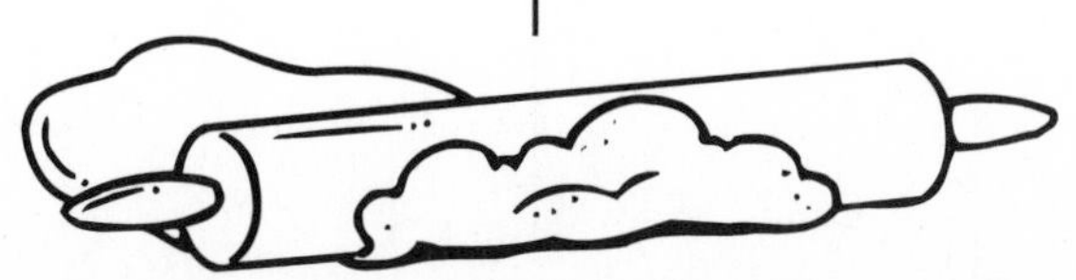

How Long?

Work each problem.

12 inches = 1 foot	3 feet = 1 yard
1 yard = 36 inches	1 mile = 5,280 feet

Kenny buys 21 feet of string. How many yards of string does he buy? **21 ÷ 3 = 7 yards of string**

1. Sami buys 9 yards of fabric. How many feet of fabric does she have?

2. Maria needs 72 feet of ribbon for her project. How many yards of ribbon should she buy?

3. Cameron is 5 feet and 9 inches tall. How many inches tall is Cameron?

4. Peter runs 10,560 feet. How many miles does he run?

How Long?

Work each problem.

1. Tim buys fencing for his dog pen that measures 9 feet on each side. The pen has 4 sides. How many inches of fencing does Tim buy altogether?

2. Jane buys 5 yards of blue fabric. Then she buys 2 feet of red fabric and 4 feet of green fabric. How many inches of fabric does Jane buy altogether?

3. Eddie is 6 feet 2 inches tall. His brother is 4 feet 9 inches tall. How much taller in inches is Eddie than his brother?

4. Maya's square quilt measures 99 inches on each edge. How many yards of trim does she need to buy to go around the entire quilt?

Sports-R-Us

Work each problem.

Jen boxes soccer balls. She puts 12 balls in each box. If she has 276 soccer balls, how many boxes does she have?

23 boxes

$$\begin{array}{r} 23 \\ 12\overline{)276} \\ \underline{-24} \\ 36 \\ \underline{-36} \\ 0 \end{array}$$

1. George boxes basketballs at the Sports-R-Us store. He puts 13 basketballs in each box. If he has 117 basketballs, how many boxes will he need?

2. Rachell packages tennis balls. She puts 24 tennis balls in each package. If she has 360 tennis balls, how many packages can she make?

3. Donna has 1,302 footballs to put on shelves. If she has 31 shelves, how many footballs can she put on each shelf?

4. The Sports-R-Us store sold 936 golf balls. If each package had 12 golf balls in it, how many packages did the store sell?

Sports-R-Us

Work each problem.

1. George packages golf balls in packages of 6. He has 348 golf balls. If he sells a 6-pack of golf balls for $1.75, how much will he make selling all of the golf balls?

2. Matt boxes skateboards. He has 253 green skateboards, 239 blue skateboards, and 180 purple skateboards. If he puts 12 skateboards in each box, how many boxes does he have?

3. Lori has 125 orange dumbbells, 83 yellow dumbbells, and 144 black dumbbells to put on shelves in the store. If she has 32 shelves, how many dumbbells can she put on each shelf?

4. Alexis puts 8 soccer balls in each box. She has 552 soccer balls. She has 574 footballs and puts 7 in each box. How many more boxes of footballs than soccer balls does Alexis have?

Time Travel

Work each problem.

1 year = 12 months	24 hours = 1 day
7 days = 1 week	60 minutes = 1 hour
Tim hiked for 240 minutes. How many hours did he spend hiking?	**240 ÷ 60 = 4 hours**

1. Allie went on vacation for 28 days. How many weeks was she on vacation?

2. Tanner's flight was 180 minutes. How many hours did he spend flying?

3. If Eric drove for 144 hours, how many days did he spend driving?

4. Robyn traveled for 36 months. How many years did she travel?

Time Travel

Work each problem.

Lori rode the bus each day for 5 weeks. If the bus costs \$1.29 per day to ride, how much did Lori spend altogether?	**5 x 7 = 35 days Lori rode the bus** **\$1.29 per day** **x 35 days** **645** **+ 3,870** **\$45.15**

1. Ryan drove 129 minutes on Monday. He drove 98 minutes on Tuesday and 73 minutes on Wednesday. How many hours did Ryan spend driving altogether?

2. Rachell took a cruise for 42 days. If the cruise cost \$124.89 per week, how much did she spend on her cruise?

3. Callie drove for 540 minutes. If she traveled 65 miles per hour, how many miles did she travel total?

4. Jason rode his bike for 360 minutes. If he traveled 2 miles per hour, how many miles did he travel?

Hitting the High Notes

Work each problem using the circle graph.

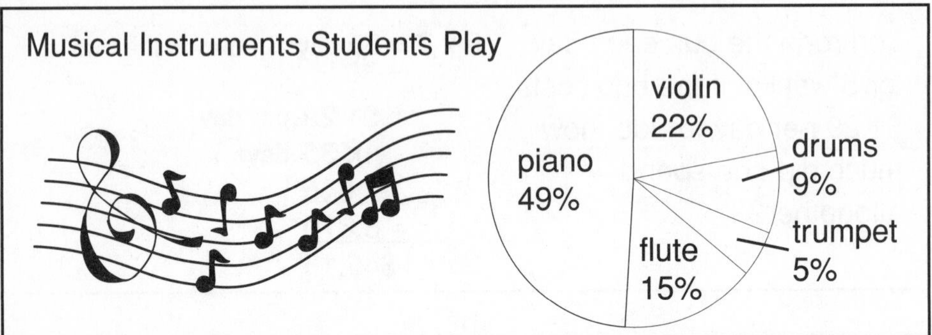

1. What instrument do the most students play?

2. What percentage of students play the drums?

3. What instrument do the least number of students play?

4. What percentage of students play the violin or flute?

Snow Sports

Lori's class voted on their favorite winter sport. Work each problem using the circle graph.

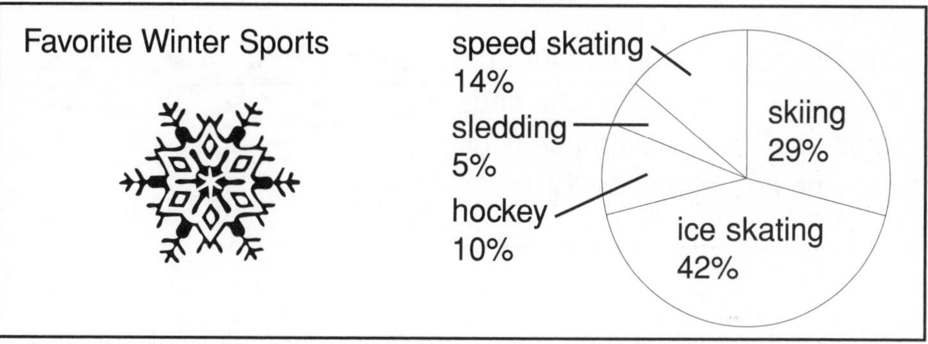

1. What winter sport do the most students like?

2. What percentage of students voted for speed skating?

3. What was the least favorite sport?

4. How many more students voted for ice skating than skiing? Give your answer as a percentage.

Kitchen Fractions

Emilee and her friends are making treats for the bake sale at their school. Help them solve each problem.

George puts $\frac{1}{3}$ cup of flour in the cookie dough. Then he adds another $\frac{2}{3}$ cup. How much flour does he add altogether?

$\frac{1}{3} + \frac{2}{3} = \frac{3}{3}$ or 1 cup

1. Greta puts $\frac{3}{4}$ cup of oatmeal in the dough. She adds another $1\frac{1}{4}$ cups. How many cups of oatmeal did Greta add altogether?

2. Lori measures $2\frac{3}{4}$ cups of chocolate chips and puts them in a bowl. Then she takes out $1\frac{1}{4}$ cups. How many chocolate chips does she have in her bowl now?

3. Grayson's bag of sugar has $5\frac{5}{8}$ cups in it. He uses $2\frac{3}{8}$ cups. How much sugar is left in his bag?

4. Denise puts $1\frac{1}{4}$ teaspoons of vanilla in the dough. Then she adds another $\frac{3}{4}$ teaspoon. How many teaspoons of vanilla does Denise use altogether?

Kitchen Fractions

Solve each problem. Remember to include the correct measurement in your answer.

1 tablespoon = 3 teaspoons   1 pint = 2 cups
1 quart = 2 pints   1 gallon = 4 quarts
1 pound = 16 ounces

Emma measures $1\frac{2}{3}$ quarts of cherries and $\frac{1}{3}$ quart of peaches. How many *pints* of fruit did Emma measure altogether?

$1\frac{2}{3} + \frac{1}{3} =$
$\frac{5}{3} + \frac{1}{3} =$
$\frac{6}{3}$ = 2 quarts
2 quarts = 4 pints of fruit

1. Matt puts $3\frac{1}{2}$ quarts of lemonade in the pitcher. He adds another $\frac{1}{2}$ quart. How many pints of lemonade does he have total?

2. Cheiko bottles $4\frac{1}{8}$ quarts of root beer. Then she bottles another $5\frac{7}{8}$ quarts of root beer. How many 1-cup servings of root beer does she have?

3. Allison measures $1\frac{5}{16}$ teaspoons of salt. She measures another $1\frac{11}{16}$ teaspoons of salt. How many tablespoons does she measure altogether?

4. Robyn has $6\frac{2}{3}$ pounds of cheese. She buys another $2\frac{1}{3}$ pounds of cheese. How many ounces of cheese does Robyn have total?

Weighing In

Work each problem. Remember to write your answer in simplest form.

Dexter has 2 boxes of oranges that weigh a total of $5\frac{1}{3}$ pounds. The first box weighs $3\frac{1}{2}$ pounds. How much does the second box weigh?

$$5\frac{1}{3} - 3\frac{1}{2} =$$
$$\frac{16}{3} - \frac{7}{2} =$$
$$\frac{32}{6} - \frac{21}{6} =$$
$$\frac{11}{6} = 1\frac{5}{6} \textbf{ pounds}$$

1. Kim has two packages to mail. Her packages weigh $6\frac{1}{8}$ pounds total. If her first package weighs $4\frac{1}{2}$ pounds, how much does her second package weigh?

2. Stuart's recipe calls for $5\frac{1}{4}$ cups of chocolate chips. He puts in $2\frac{1}{3}$ cups. How many more cups of chocolate chips does he need?

3. Alan weighs $73\frac{1}{3}$ pounds. Chris weighs $61\frac{1}{2}$ pounds. How much more does Alan weigh than Chris?

4. Jasmine and her friend get on the big scale at the amusement park. Jasmine weighs $55\frac{1}{2}$ pounds, and her friend weighs $62\frac{1}{4}$ pounds. How many pounds do they weigh altogether?

Weighing In

Work each problem.

Bruce is shipping 2 cartons. His cartons weigh $3\frac{3}{4}$ pounds and $7\frac{1}{2}$ pounds. If shipping costs $1.15 per pound, approximately how much will it cost Bruce to ship his cartons?

$$3\frac{3}{4} + 7\frac{1}{2} =$$
$$\frac{15}{4} + \frac{15}{2} =$$
$$\frac{15}{4} + \frac{30}{4} =$$
$$\frac{45}{4} = 11\frac{1}{4}$$

11 x $1.15 = $12.65

(It would cost a little more than $12.65.)

1. Marcus has 3 bags of marbles that weigh $7\frac{5}{8}$ pounds altogether. The first bag weighs $3\frac{1}{4}$ pounds, and the second bag weighs $2\frac{1}{8}$ pounds. How much does the third bag weigh?

2. At the grocery store, the butcher puts $1\frac{1}{2}$ pounds of meat on the scale. She adds $4\frac{3}{4}$ pounds more. How much does the meat weigh altogether? If the meat costs $3.69 per pound, approximately how much will it cost?

3. Elena buys $6\frac{1}{2}$ pounds of candy altogether. She buys $1\frac{1}{4}$ pounds of licorice and $2\frac{1}{8}$ pounds of gumdrops. How many pounds of lemon drops does she buy?

4. Erin buys $2\frac{1}{4}$ pounds of nails. Then she goes back and buys another $3\frac{1}{2}$ pounds of nails. If nails cost $1.25 a pound, approximately how much does Erin spend?

Are We There Yet?

April's family is going on vacation. Solve each problem.

April carries 5 suitcases to the car. Each suitcase weighs $6\frac{1}{3}$ pounds. How many pounds does April carry in all?

$5 \times 6\frac{1}{3} =$

$\frac{5}{1} \times \frac{19}{3} =$

$\frac{95}{3}$ or $31\frac{2}{3}$ pounds

1. April's little brother packs 7 toys in his bag. If each toy weighs $1\frac{3}{4}$ ounces, how many ounces does his bag weigh?

2. On Monday, April's family drives $45\frac{1}{3}$ miles each hour. If they travel for 9 hours, how many miles do they travel altogether?

3. Each person drinks $8\frac{1}{3}$ ounces of soda. If there are 5 people in April's family, how many ounces of soda do they drink altogether?

4. April's mom buys 4 souvenirs. If each souvenir weighs $7\frac{5}{8}$ grams, how many grams do they weigh altogether?

Are We There Yet?

Work each problem.

1. On Wednesday, April's family travels 64 $\frac{1}{4}$ miles each hour. If they travel for 8 hours, how many miles do they travel altogether?

2. April listens to CDs. If she listens to 3 $\frac{1}{5}$ CDs each hour, how many CDs does she listen to in 4 hours?

3. If April's family can drive 23 $\frac{1}{8}$ miles on 1 gallon of gas, how far can they drive on 17 gallons?

4. A truck leaves the gas station the same time April's family does. The truck travels 75 $\frac{1}{2}$ miles per hour. April's family travels 65 $\frac{1}{2}$ miles per hour. How many miles more will the truck have traveled than April's family in 6 hours?

Around Town

Work each problem using the map below.

Alan rides the bus from the library to school and then to the museum. How many miles does Alan travel altogether?	$2\frac{2}{3} + 3\frac{3}{4} = \frac{8}{3} + \frac{15}{4} = \frac{32}{12} + \frac{45}{12} = \frac{77}{12}$ or $6\frac{5}{12}$ miles

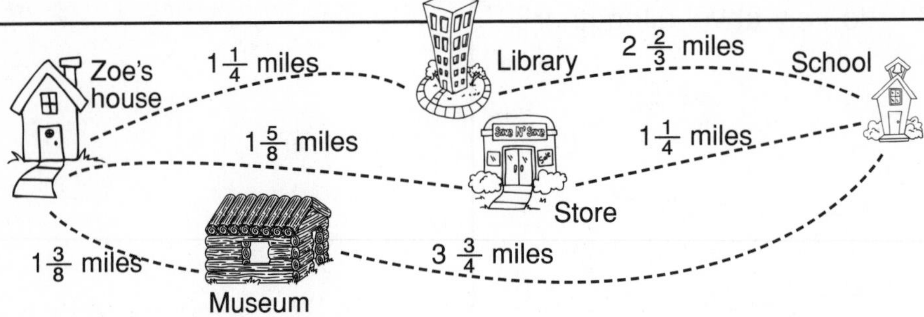

1. Zoe took the bus from her house to the store and then to school. How far did Zoe ride altogether?

2. Tim walked from Zoe's house to the store and then back to Zoe's house. How far did Tim walk?

3. Alex drove 3 times as far as Christine. If Christine drove from the library to school and then to the store, how far did Alex drive?

4. Eddie walked from the museum to Zoe's house and then to the store. Allison walked from the museum to school. How much farther did Allison walk than Eddie?

Around Town

Work each problem using the map below.

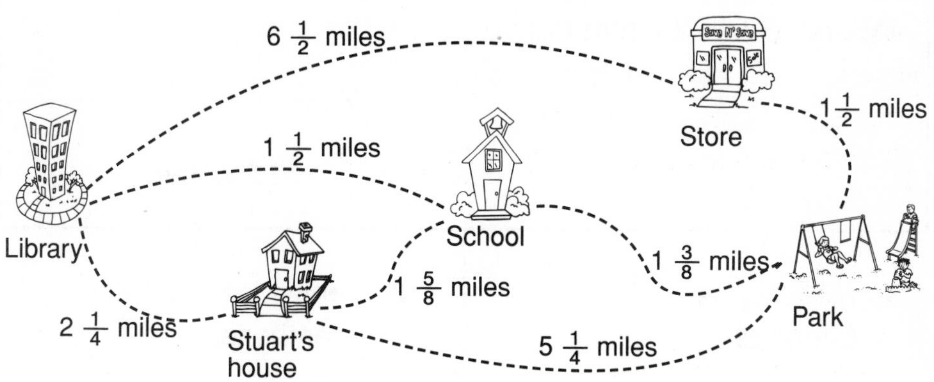

1. Lori jogged from the library to Stuart's house. Emilee jogged 5 times as many miles as Lori. How many miles did Emilee jog?

2. Tess lives 6 times as many miles away from school as Stuart does. How many miles from school does Tess live?

3. Grayson ran from Stuart's house to the park and then to the store. How far did he run altogether?

4. Amy traveled 8 times as many miles as Stuart. If Stuart drove from his house to the school and then to the park, how many miles did Amy travel?

Decimal Distances

Write the decimal number from each sentence.

Jack ran 3 and 2-tenths miles.

3.2 miles

1. Matt traveled 2 and 6-tenths meters.

2. Denise jogged 4 and 4-tenths feet.

3. Emilee skated 8 and 7-tenths miles.

4. Grayson biked 13 and 9-tenths miles.

Decimal Distances

Write the decimal number from each sentence.

Tyler drove 7 and 2-hundredths miles.

7.02 miles

1. Eden ran 2 and 6-hundredths meters.

2. Sara drove 41 and 4-hundredths miles.

3. Mike raced 89 and 13-hundredths miles.

4. Chris swam 13 and 24-hundredths meters.

Decimal Distances

Write the decimal number from each sentence.

Kaylee rode her scooter 6 and 4-thousandths miles.

6.004 miles

1. Emilee ran the race in 9 and 3-thousandths seconds.

2. Rachell traveled 14 and 58-thousandths miles.

3. Grayson drove 124 and 73-thousandths miles.

4. Lori skied 12 and 9-thousandths meters.

Tipping the Scale

Solve each problem.

Gary's box weighs 45.38 pounds. Meg's box weighs 13.93 pounds. How many more pounds does Gary's box weigh than Meg's?

$$\begin{array}{r} \overset{4}{4}\overset{1}{\not{5}}.38 \\ -\ 13.93 \\ \hline 31.45 \end{array}$$

31.45 pounds more

1. Natalie weighs 64.043 pounds. Her sister weighs 43.39 pounds. How many more pounds does Natalie weigh than her sister?

2. Matt buys 12.842 pounds of long nails. Then he buys 38.473 pounds of short nails. How many pounds of nails does Matt buy in all?

3. Rachell catches a fish that weighs 15.002 ounces. Grayson catches a fish that weighs 21.842 ounces. How many ounces do the fish weigh altogether?

4. Steven's bag of candy weighs 5.932 grams. Sara's bag of candy weighs 3.803 grams. How many more grams does Steven's bag weigh?

Racetrack Racers

Work each problem.

The red racecar drove 6.9 laps. The blue racecar drove 5.5 times as many laps as the red racecar. How many laps did the blue racecar drive?	6.9 x 5.5 345 + 3450 37.95 **laps**	There are 2 numbers behind the decimals in the problem, so there are 2 numbers behind the decimal in the answer.

1. Jeff raced 4.8 times as many laps as Mark. If Mark raced 3.7 laps, how many laps did Jeff race?

2. Denise finished the race in 5.93 minutes. If Tanner took 4.6 times as long to finish the race, how many minutes did it take him to finish?

3. Tyler used 17.04 gallons of gas. Marta used 6.2 times as many gallons of gas as Tyler. How many gallons of gas did Marta use?

4. Grayson ran 2.4 times as many miles as Emilee. If Emilee ran 2.08 miles, how many miles did Grayson run?

Racetrack Racers

Work each problem.

1. Rob's finishing time was 3.4 times as long as Matt's finishing time. If Matt's finishing time was 10.48 minutes, what was Rob's finishing time?

2. Lori ran 6.2 times as many laps as Denise. If Denise ran 8.7 laps, how many laps did Lori run?

3. Jasmine finished the race in 18.6 minutes. If Becky took 2.7 times as long to finish the race, how many minutes did it take her to finish?

4. Tim's racecar can go 22.93 miles on 1 gallon of gas. How many miles can his racecar go on 15.5 gallons of gas?

Cosmic Cuisine

Use the menu to solve each problem.

Menu Item	Price
Cosmic Burger	$4.26
Saturn Sandwich	$2.19
Solar Shake	$1.79
Jupiter Juice	$.89
Galactic Garden Salad	$5.49
Earth Potato	$.99
Mars Munches	$6.79
Pluto Pie	$3.75

Alan buys a Cosmic Burger and a Jupiter Juice. How much does he spend altogether?

$$\begin{array}{r} \scriptstyle 1\,1 \\ \$4.26 \\ +\ \ .89 \\ \hline \$5.15 \end{array}$$

1. George has $20.25 in his pocket. If he buys a Saturn Sandwich, a Solar Shake, and an Earth Potato, how much will he have left?

2. Lori buys 2 Pluto Pies and a Jupiter Juice. How much does she spend altogether?

3. Emilio orders a Solar Shake and 2 Earth Potatoes. He gives the clerk $5.00. How much change does he get back?

4. Dylan goes through the drive-thru and buys 15 Saturn Sandwiches. How much does he spend?

Cosmic Cuisine

Use the menu on the previous page to solve each problem.

1. Ed buys a Galactic Garden Salad and a Jupiter Juice. How much does he spend in all?

2. Denise buys 6 Cosmic Burgers and a Solar Shake. Matt buys 4 Saturn Sandwiches, 2 Earth Potatoes, and a Pluto Pie. Who spends more, Denise or Matt? How much more is spent?

3. Tara orders 3 Galactic Garden Salads, a Cosmic Burger, and a Solar Shake. She pays with $25.00. How much change does she get back?

4. Emilee buys 17 Earth Potatoes and 3 Pluto Pies. How much does she spend altogether?

Popular Pet Names

Use the circle graph to answer each question.

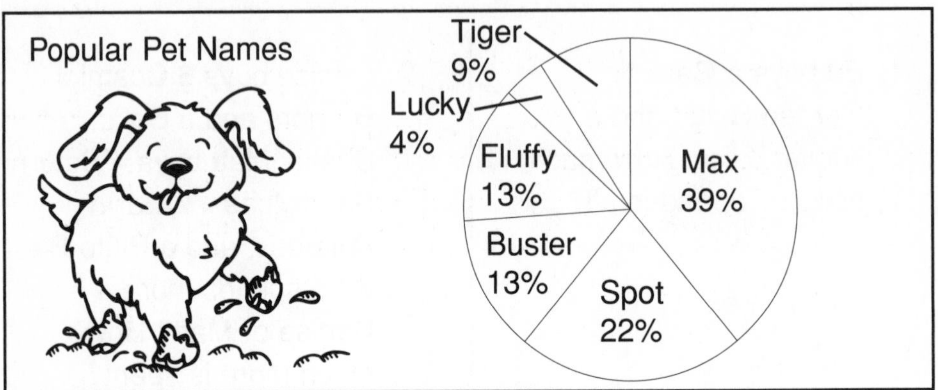

1. What is the most popular pet name?

2. What percent of pets are named Lucky or Tiger?

3. What is the least popular pet name?

4. What percent of pets are named Spot?

Movie Ticket Sales

Use the information in the table to answer each question.

Theater Tickets Sold				
	January	February	March	April
Cinemania Theater	2,489	1,509	908	580
Showtown Theater	3,587	2,687	1,788	679
MovieMax Theater	1,007	814	498	466

1. How many tickets did the Showtown Theater sell in March?

2. How many tickets were sold in February altogether?

3. How many more tickets did the Showtown Theater sell than the Cinemania Theater in January?

4. If a movie ticket costs $5.49, how much did the Cinemania Theater earn in March and April?

Metric Measures

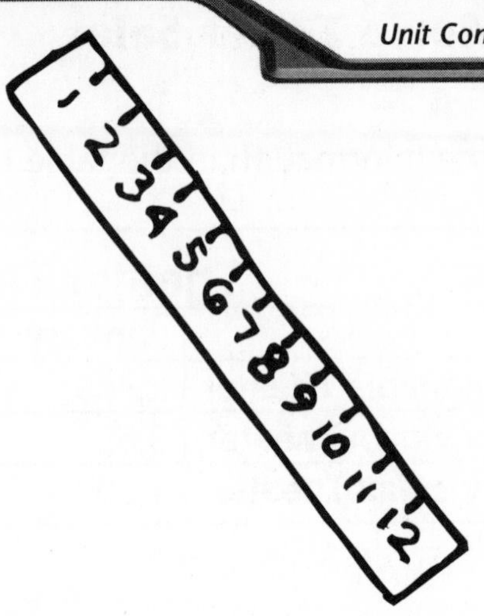

Solve each problem.

1 kilometer = 1,000 meters
1 meter = 100 centimeters

1 liter = 1,000 milliliters
1 kiloliter = 1,000 liters

1 gram = 1,000 milligrams
1 kilogram = 1,000 grams

Carter measures 60 meters of ribbon. How many centimeters of ribbon does Carter have? **60 x 100 = 6,000 centimeters**

1. Rachell measures 40 meters of string. How many centimeters of string does she have?

2. Matt's box weighs 45 grams. How many milligrams does his box weigh?

3. Linus measures 5,000 liters of lemonade. How many kiloliters of lemonade does Linus have?

4. Allie ran 10 meters. How many centimeters did she run?

Metric Measures

Solve each problem.

1. Matt measures 3 pieces of string. The first piece is 544 cm. The second piece is 144 cm, and the third piece is 112 cm. How many meters of string does he have altogether?

2. Grayson made 12,000 milliliters of root beer. If he sells 1-liter bottles for $1.09, how much will he earn?

3. Nicole is shipping 2 boxes. The first box weighs 4,180 g, and the second box weighs 820 g. If shipping costs $6.43 per kilogram, how much does Nicole spend on shipping?

4. Anna bottled 47,000 milliliters of punch. If she sells 1-liter bottles for $1.79, how much will she make?

Bike and Scooter Sales

Use the line graph to answer each question.

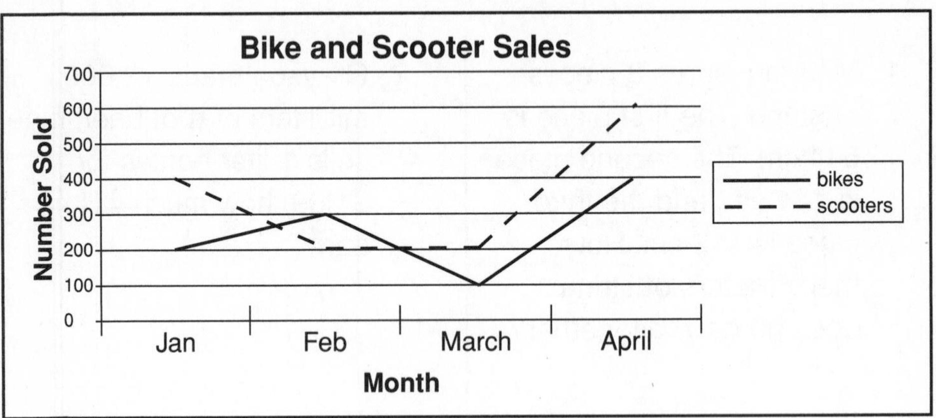

1. How many total bikes and scooters were sold in January?

2. In which months were the least number of scooters sold?

3. How many more scooters than bikes were sold during the 4-month period?

4. If bikes cost $89.58 each, how much did the store make during March and April in bike sales?

At the Amusement Park

Use the bar graph to answer each question.

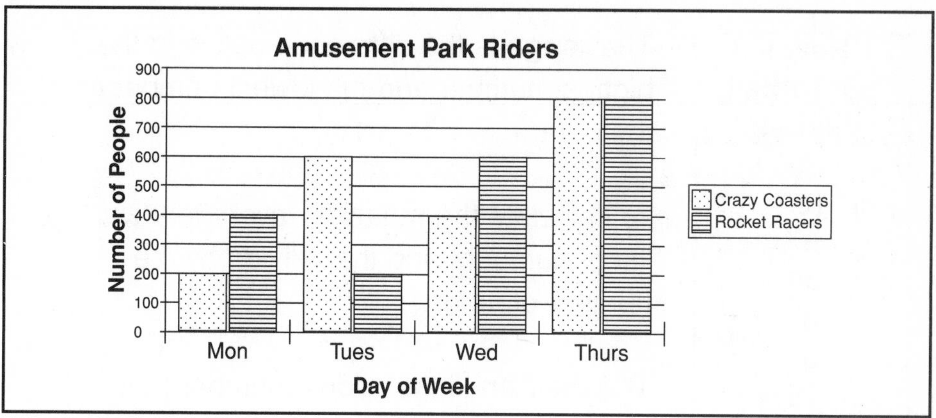

1. How many people rode the Rocket Racers on Tuesday?

2. What day of the week did the same number of people ride the Crazy Coaster and Rocket Racers?

3. What was the total number of people who rode the Crazy Coaster during the 4-day period?

4. If the park charged $1.35 per ride, how much money did they make from people who rode the Rocket Racers during the last 4 days?

Through the Hoop

Use the chart to answer the questions.

Bear's Basketball Scores
107
102
97
89
88
87
79
79
75
74
69

The **range** is the difference between the highest number and the lowest number in the data.

To calculate the **mean** (or average), add the list of numbers and then divide by the number of items.

The **median** is the middle number that appears in the data.

The **mode** is the number that appears most often in the data.

1. What is the **range** of the data?

2. What is the **mode** of the data?

3. What is the **median** of the data?

4. What is the **mean** of the points scored?

Weather Watching

Use the chart to answer the questions.

Inches of Rainfall
6.5
6.2
5.4
5.3
3.0
3.0
2.9
2.7
1.9

The **range** is the difference between the highest number and the lowest number in the data.

To calculate the **mean** (or average), add the list of numbers and then divide by the number of items.

The **median** is the middle number that appears in the data.

The **mode** is the number that appears most often in the data.

1. What is the **range** of the data?

2. What is the **mode** of the data?

3. What is the **median** of the data?

4. What is the **mean** of the inches of rainfall?

Perfect Pizza

Lucy and her friends are making pizzas for a fundraiser. Help them solve each problem.

1. Lori needs 224 ounces of cheese. How many pounds should she buy?

2. Emilee sells 23 times as many pizzas as Rachell. If Rachell sells 15 pizzas, how many pizzas does Emilee sell?

3. Each pizza needs 1 cup of tomato sauce. Lucy makes 244 pizzas. If tomato sauce is $2.59 a quart, how much does Lucy spend?

4. Tim makes 241 pepperoni pizzas, 484 cheese pizzas, and 187 vegetable pizzas. If Tim cuts each pizza into 12 slices, how many slices does he have altogether?

Perfect Pizza

Work each problem.

1. Jamie boxes 732 pizzas in a week. She boxes 172 pizzas on Monday and 109 pizzas on Tuesday. How many pizzas does she box the rest of the week?

2. Allison has 4 bags of pepperoni. Each bag has 162 pieces of pepperoni. If she puts 27 pieces of pepperoni on each pizza, how many pizzas can she make?

3. Grayson carries 7 packages of cheese to the kitchen. Each package weighs $5\frac{1}{8}$ pounds. How many pounds does Grayson carry altogether?

4. Lori's group sells 583 pizzas. If each pizza sells for $3.59, how much money does Lori's group make?

At the Fair

Read each problem and decide if enough information is given to solve it. If there is enough information, solve the problem.

1. Justin buys 4 hot dogs for $1.69 and 7 tickets for $8.49. How much change does he get back?

2. Grayson rides the Ferris wheel 5 times. One ride takes 3 tickets. If one ticket costs $1.35, how much does Grayson spend altogether?

3. Kim buys a T-shirt and Stacy buys a snow cone. Snow cones are $.65 each. How much do Kim and Stacy spend altogether?

4. Lori buys 4 tickets for $2.59 each and cotton candy for $2.49. She gives the cashier $20.00. How much change does she get back?

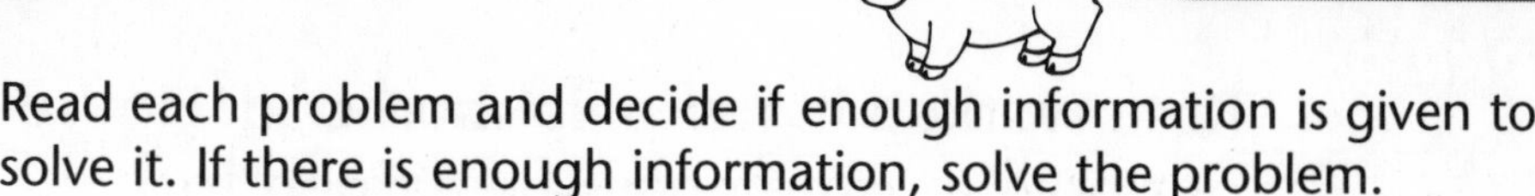

At the Fair

Mixed Practice

Read each problem and decide if enough information is given to solve it. If there is enough information, solve the problem.

1. Tanner sees 3 times as many cows as horses at the fair. He sees 12 pigs. How many animals does he see in all?

2. Jenny sells 4,392 tickets for the fair in one week. She sells 1,382 tickets on Monday, 809 on Tuesday, and 455 on Wednesday. How many tickets does she sell the rest of the week?

3. Lori makes jam for the fair. She uses $4\frac{5}{8}$ cups of sugar and then adds another $1\frac{2}{3}$ cups. How much sugar does she use altogether?

4. Sara buys a soda for $2.29 and 2 slices of pizza. If she pays with $10.00, how much change does she get back?

Critical Thinking Skills

Odd Jobs

Rosa worked in her neighborhood. Figure out how much money she earned for each job she did.

Rosa earned $16.46 for babysitting.

She earned 3 times as much for cleaning the garage as she did for babysitting.

She earned $24.88 less for raking leaves as she did for cleaning the garage.

She earned $\frac{1}{2}$ as much for washing dishes as she did for babysitting.

She earned $15.79 more for washing the car than she did for washing dishes.

She earned 2 times as much for mowing the lawn as she did for washing the car.

Job:	**Amount:**
Babysitting	**1.**
Mowing lawn	**2.**
Raking leaves	**3.**
Washing dishes	**4.**
Cleaning garage	**5.**
Washing car	**6.**

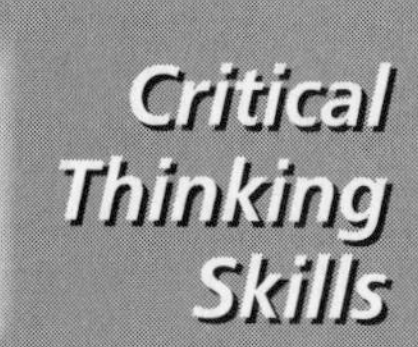

Odd Jobs

Work each problem. Use the information in the table on the previous page.

1. How much did Rosa earn washing the car and the dishes?

2. How much more did Rosa earn from cleaning the garage than babysitting?

3. What was the total amount Rosa earned?

4. Rosa is saving for a new bike that costs $189.00. How much more does she need to earn before she has enough?

Critical Thinking Skills

Car Sales

Figure out how much each person paid for his or her car. Make a table to help organize the information.

Christie paid 3 times as much as Jamie.

Chad paid $19,348 less than Liz.

Rex paid $32,938 for his car.

Jamie paid $4,258 less than Mick paid.

Liz paid $1,978 less than Christie.

Mick paid $\frac{1}{2}$ as much as Rex paid.

Person:	Price Paid:
Christie	**1.**
Chad	**2.**
Rex	**3.**
Jamie	**4.**
Liz	**5.**
Mick	**6.**

Car Sales

Critical Thinking Skills

Work each problem. Use the information in the table on the previous page.

1. What is the difference between the highest price paid and the lowest price paid?

2. If Christie makes the same monthly payment for 1 year to pay off the car, how much is each payment?

3. Liz has $22,495 for her car. She needs to borrow the rest of the money from the bank. How much will she need to borrow?

4. Rex's car goes down in value each year. He figures that the value decreases $1,693 each year. How much will his car be worth in 5 years?

Critical Thinking Skills

Auction Items

Carlos went to an auction. Help him figure out the price of each auction item.

The desk cost $1,584.02 more than the vase.

The painting cost 21 times as much as the lamp.

The vase cost $309 less than the painting.

The lamp cost $65.38.

The watch cost $\frac{1}{4}$ as much as the desk.

The car cost 24 times as much as the painting.

Item:	**Cost:**
Lamp	**1.**
Car	**2.**
Vase	**3.**
Painting	**4.**
Desk	**5.**
Watch	**6.**

Auction Items

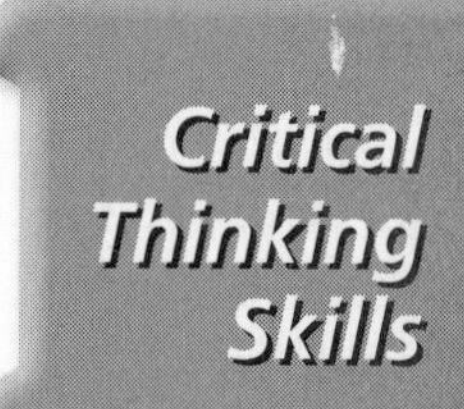

Use the answers from the previous page to solve each problem.

1. What is the difference in cost between the highest- and lowest-priced items?

2. There were 3 bids for the desk: $2,648, $1,489, and $2,421. What was the average of the bids?

3. How much more did the painting sell for than the vase?

4. The value of the painting goes up $769 each year. How much will the painting be worth in 7 years?

Critical Thinking Skills

Video Game Scores

Amanda and her friends are playing their favorite video game. Figure out how many points each earned.

Kim earned 609 fewer points than Stuart.

Jan earned 9 times as many points as Amanda.

Amanda earned 793 points.

Maria earned $\frac{1}{2}$ as many points as Tim.

Stuart earned 4 times as many points as Maria.

Tim earned 1,213 more points than Amanda.

Name:	**Points Scored:**
Amanda	**1.**
Jan	**2.**
Tim	**3.**
Maria	**4.**
Stuart	**5.**
Kim	**6.**

Answer Pages

Page 3
1. 201 chocolates
2. 207 candy bars
3. 167 pounds
4. 196 pieces

Page 4
1. 2,050 shoes
2. 2,061 sneakers
3. 1,949 inches
4. 1,697 bottles

Page 5
1. 15,856 shoe boxes
2. 1,927 flip-flops
3. 13,380 boots
4. 1,351 shoes

Page 6
1. 7,102 pages
2. 578 pages
3. 5,496 pages
4. 1,764 pages

Page 7
1. 570 pages
2. 7,245 pages
3. 584 pages
4. 11,601 pages

Page 8
1. 2,331 people
2. 128,630 people

Page 9
1. Miami Beach; Jackson, Mississippi
2. 63,243 people
3. Newport Beach
4. 343,846 people

Page 10
1. 1,338 wildflowers
2. 3,049 supplies
3. 765 squirrels and chipmunks
4. 6,321 campers

Page 11
1. 291 animal pictures
2. 101 campers
3. 125 tents
4. 976 bags

Page 12
1. 243 meatballs
2. 802 customers
3. 37 customers
4. $12.29

Page 13
1. 263 pounds
2. $8.88
3. 131 loaves
4. $254.83

Page 14
1. 4,401 tickets
2. 17,817 tickets
3. 3,288 tickets
4. 38,664 tickets

Page 15
1. 2,151 people
2. 772 tickets
3. 2,096 tickets
4. 19,328 tickets

Page 16
1. $252.89
2. $75.75
3. 1,100 cards
4. $1,043

Page 17
1. 4,494 marbles
2. $711.40
3. 24,003 cans
4. $259.92

Page 18
1. 48 servings
2. 64 quarts
3. 3 pounds
4. 16 servings

Page 19
1. 4 pounds
2. 24 servings
3. 48 pints
4. 32 servings

Page 20
1. 1,392 pizzas
2. 2,294 nails
3. 1,472 baseballs
4. 1,674 stickers

Page 21
1. 4,736 T-shirts
2. 8,378 cars
3. 464 diapers
4. 5,192 books

Page 22
1. $13.00
2. $66.39
3. $7.12
4. $2.33

Page 23
1. $2.50
2. $10.86
3. $23.15
4. $92.87

Page 24
1. 282 feet
2. 1,494 feet
3. 592 feet
4. 86 feet; $6.02

Page 25
1. 564 feet
2. 396 inches
3. 566 feet
4. 1,588 feet; $397.00

Page 26
1. 1,728 square inches
2. 17,640 square inches
3. 276 square feet
4. 1,768 square feet

Answer Pages

Page 27
1. 8,722 square inches
2. 93 pints
3. 970 square feet
4. 187 bags

Page 28
1. 99 bags
2. 69 crates
3. 31 boxes
4. 78 bunches

Page 29
1. $16.90
2. 133 bags with 29 limes left over
3. 196 bunches with 3 avocados left over
4. 257 bags

Page 30
1. 1,482 packages with 4 cookies left over
2. 822 boxes
3. 487 boxes with 6 bagels left over
4. 647 cakes

Page 31
1. 409 boxes with 1 donut left over
2. 454 packages with 6 rolls left over
3. 652 containers with 7 cookies left over
4. $789.70

Page 32
1. 27 feet
2. 24 yards
3. 69 inches
4. 2 miles

Page 33
1. 432 inches
2. 252 inches
3. 17 inches
4. 11 yards

Page 34
1. 9 boxes
2. 15 packages
3. 42 footballs
4. 78 packages

Page 35
1. $101.50
2. 56 boxes
3. 11 dumbbells
4. 13 boxes

Page 36
1. 4 weeks
2. 3 hours
3. 6 days
4. 3 years

Page 37
1. 5 hours
2. $749.34
3. 585 miles
4. 12 miles

Page 38
1. piano
2. 9%
3. trumpet
4. 37%

Answer Pages

Page 39
1. ice skating
2. 14%
3. sledding
4. 13%

Page 40
1. 2 cups
2. $1\frac{2}{4}$ or $1\frac{1}{2}$ cups
3. $3\frac{2}{8}$ or $3\frac{1}{4}$ cups
4. 2 teaspoons

Page 41
1. 8 pints
2. 40 cups
3. 1 tablespoon
4. 144 ounces

Page 42
1. $1\frac{5}{8}$ pounds
2. $2\frac{11}{12}$ cups
3. $11\frac{5}{6}$ pounds
4. $117\frac{3}{4}$ pounds

Page 43
1. $2\frac{1}{4}$ pounds
2. $6\frac{1}{4}$ pounds, a little more than $23
3. $3\frac{1}{8}$ pounds
4. between $6.25 and $7.50

Page 44
1. $12\frac{1}{4}$ ounces
2. 408 miles
3. $41\frac{2}{3}$ ounces
4. $30\frac{1}{2}$ grams

Page 45
1. 514 miles
2. $12\frac{4}{5}$ CDs
3. $393\frac{1}{8}$ miles
4. 60 miles more

Page 46
1. $2\frac{7}{8}$ miles
2. $3\frac{1}{4}$ miles
3. $11\frac{3}{4}$ miles
4. $\frac{3}{4}$ mile

Page 47
1. $11\frac{1}{4}$ miles
2. $9\frac{3}{4}$ miles
3. $6\frac{3}{4}$ miles
4. 24 miles

Page 48
1. 2.6 meters
2. 4.4 feet
3. 8.7 miles
4. 13.9 miles

Page 49
1. 2.06 meters
2. 41.04 miles
3. 89.13 miles
4. 13.24 meters

Page 50
1. 9.003 seconds
2. 14.058 miles
3. 124.073 miles
4. 12.009 meters

Answer Pages

Page 51
1. 20.653 pounds
2. 51.315 pounds
3. 36.844 ounces
4. 2.129 grams

Page 52
1. 17.76 laps
2. 27.278 minutes
3. 105.648 gallons
4. 4.992 miles

Page 53
1. 35.632 minutes
2. 53.94 laps
3. 50.22 minutes
4. 355.415 miles

Page 54
1. $15.28
2. $8.39
3. $1.23
4. $32.85

Page 55
1. $6.38
2. Denise, $12.86 more
3. $2.48
4. $28.08

Page 56
1. Max
2. 13%
3. Lucky
4. 22%

Page 57
1. 1,788 tickets
2. 5,010 tickets
3. 1,098 tickets
4. $8,169.12

Page 58
1. 4,000 centimeters
2. 45,000 milligrams
3. 5 kiloliters
4. 1,000 centimeters

Page 59
1. 8 meters
2. $13.08
3. $32.15
4. $84.13

Page 60
1. 600 bikes and scooters
2. February and March
3. 400 scooters
4. $44,790.00

Page 61
1. 200 people
2. Thursday
3. 2,000 people
4. $2,700.00

Page 62
1. 38
2. 79
3. 87
4. 86

Page 63
1. 4.6
2. 3.0
3. 3.0
4. 4.1

Page 64
1. 14 pounds
2. 345 pizzas
3. $157.99
4. 10,944 slices

Page 65
1. 451 pizzas
2. 24 pizzas
3. 35 $\frac{7}{8}$ pounds
4. $2,092.97

Page 66
1. not enough information
2. $20.25
3. not enough information
4. $7.15

Page 67
1. not enough information
2. 1,746 tickets
3. 6 $\frac{7}{12}$ cups
4. not enough information

Page 68
1. $16.46
2. $48.04
3. $24.50
4. $8.23
5. $49.38
6. $24.02

Page 69
1. $32.25
2. $32.92
3. $170.63
4. $18.37

Page 70
1. $36,633
2. $15,307
3. $32,938
4. $12,211
5. $34,655
6. $16,469

Page 71
1. $24,422
2. $3,052.75
3. $12,160
4. $24,473

Page 72
1. $65.38
2. $32,951.52
3. $1,063.98
4. $1,372.98
5. $2,648
6. $662

Page 73
1. $32,886.14
2. $2,186
3. $309
4. $6,755.98

Page 74
1. 793 points
2. 7,137 points
3. 2,006 points
4. 1,003 points
5. 4,012 points
6. 3,403 points